GREEN HILLS PUBLIC LIBRARY DISTRICT

3 1814 00165 6039

4-01

DATE DUE

D0571975

DEMCO

Rays

by Martha E. H. Rustad

Consulting Editor: Gail Saunders-Smith, Ph.D.

Consultant: Jody Byrum, Science Writer,
SeaWorld Education Department

Pebble Books

an imprint of Capstone Press
Mankato, Minnesota

E
597.3
RU.

Pebble Books are published by Capstone Press
151 Good Counsel Drive, P.O. Box 669, Mankato, Minnesota 56002
http://www.capstone-press.com

Copyright © 2001 Capstone Press. All rights reserved.
No part of this book may be reproduced without written permission
from the publisher. The publisher takes no responsibility for the use of any
of the materials or methods described in this book, nor for the products thereof.
Printed in the United States of America.

1 2 3 4 5 6 06 05 04 03 02 01

Library of Congress Cataloging-in-Publication Data
Rustad, Martha E. H. (Martha Elizabeth Hillman), 1975–
    Rays / by Martha E. H. Rustad.
    p. cm.—(Ocean life)
    Includes bibliographical references (p. 23) and index.
    ISBN 0-7368-0858-2
    1. Rays (Fishes)—Juvenile literature. [1. Rays (Fishes).] I. Title. II. Series.
QL638.8 .R87 2001
597.3'5—dc21

                                                              00-009862

Summary: Simple text and photographs present rays and their behavior.

Note to Parents and Teachers

The Ocean Life series supports national science standards for units on the diversity and unity of life. The series shows that animals have features that help them live in different environments. This book describes rays and illustrates how they live. The photographs support early readers in understanding the text. The repetition of words and phrases helps early readers learn new words. This book also introduces early readers to subject-specific vocabulary words, which are defined in the Words to Know section. Early readers may need assistance to read some words and to use the Table of Contents, Words to Know, Read More, Internet Sites, and Index/Word List sections of the book.

Table of Contents

GREEN HILLS PUBLIC LIBRARY DISTRICT
8611 WEST 103RD STREET
PALOS HILLS, IL 60465

4

Rays are fish.

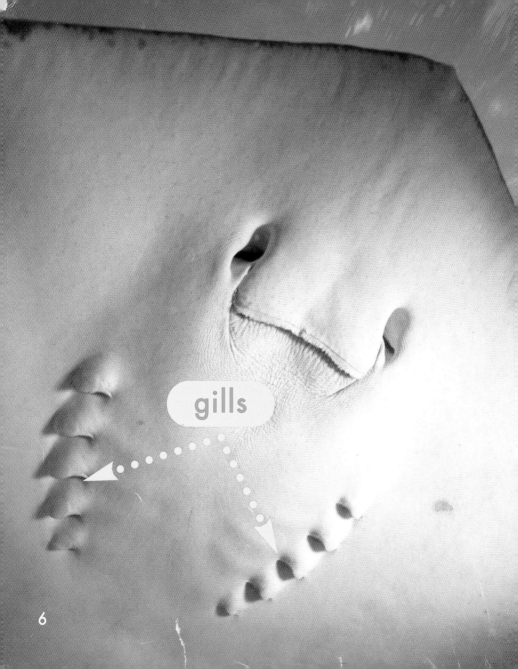

gills

Rays breathe through gills.

Rays have a flat body.

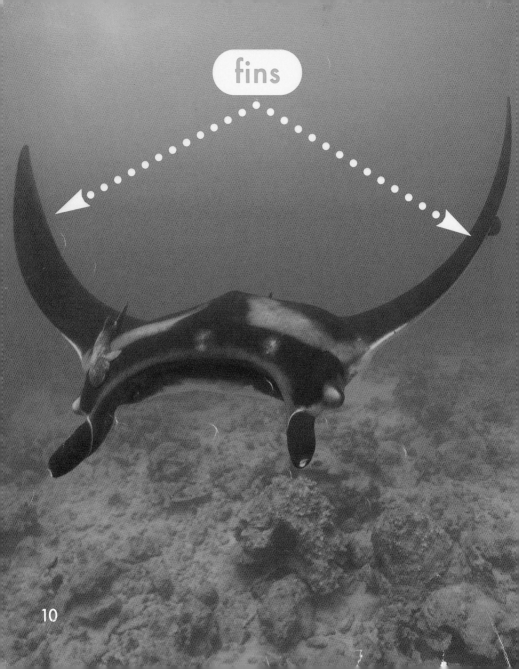

Rays have large fins
that look like wings.

tail

Most rays have a tail.

stinger

Some rays sting predators.

Rays have a mouth.

Rays eat clams,
crabs, and fish.

Most rays hunt for food near the ocean floor.

breathe—to take oxygen into the body; a ray's gills take in oxygen from the water.

fin—a body part without bones that fish use to swim; rays have two large wing-like fins that they move up and down; rays seem to fly through the water when they swim.

fish—a cold-blooded animal that lives in water and has scales, fins, and gills

gill—a body part that fish use to breathe; a ray has gills on the bottom of its flat body.

hunt—to find and kill animals for food

mouth—a body part used to take in food; most rays have hard, flat teeth.

ocean floor—the bottom of the ocean; sand, rocks, and coral reefs cover the ocean floor; rays hunt for food there.

predator—an animal that hunts and eats other animals; sharks and seals are predators of rays.

sting—to hurt with a venomous tip; some rays have a stinging spine on their tail.

Read More

Llamas, Andreu. *Rays: Animals with an Electric Charge.* Secrets of the Animal World. Milwaukee: Gareth Stevens, 1997.

Perrine, Doug. *Sharks and Rays of the World.* Stillwater, Minn.: Voyageur Press, 1999.

Seward, Homer. *Rays.* Sea Monsters. Vero Beach, Fla.: Rourke, 1998.

Internet Sites

Ray
http://kids.infoplease.com/ce6/sci/A0841237.html

Rays: Wings in the Water
http://www.aqua.org/animals/species/rays.html

What Is a Ray?
http://www.EnchantedLearning.com/subjects/sharks/rays

Index/Word List

Word Count: 48
Early-Intervention Level: 6

Credits
Steve Christensen, cover designer and illustrator; Kia Bielke, production designer;
    Kimberly Danger, photo researcher

Allan Power/Bruce Coleman Inc., 1
Graeme Teague, 18
Jay Ireland & Georgienne E. Bradley, 6, 8, 10, 12, 16, 20
Jeff Jaskolski/Innerspace Visions, cover
Norbert Wu/www.norbertwu.com, 14
Norman Owen Tomalin/Bruce Coleman Inc., 4